The Pumpkin Patch Cookbook

Forty tasty recipes celebrating the magic of pumpkin in the kitchen

by Jenny Fyall

illustrated by Annie Grant

First published by Fyall Grant in 2021
www.udnypumpkins.co.uk

Publishing services provided by Lumphanan Press
www.lumphananpress.co.uk

Illustrations © Annie Grant 2021
artbyanniegrant.co.uk

ISBN: 978-1-5272-9844-6

Printed by Imprint Digital, UK

Contents

Drinks

About us

THE BASICS

Every pumpkin is sacred!

If there is one message this recipe book aims to get across it is that no pumpkin should be wasted! In fact, no part of any pumpkin should be wasted. The whole thing can be eaten, from the flesh to the seeds and even the skin, which is actually particularly nutritious. If roasting a pumpkin whole or in slices, try leaving the skin on: it's delicious.

The recipes in this book all feature pumpkin as the main, or at least a major, ingredient. However, there are many ways to sneak small amounts of pumpkin into a meal, and in doing so add a nutritional boost. Why not grate some into a bolognaise sauce or shepherd's pie, chop some into a vegetable soup, add some to a frittata, or add some roasted pumpkin to any salad?

Even the gungy bits in the middle of the pumpkin can be used. Try chopping them up a bit and adding them into a bread mix (this works well with rye bread). It doesn't matter if a few seeds make it in too, and you can even grate in some of the skin.

In numbers

Sadly about 18,000 tonnes of pumpkin are thrown away each year in the UK and currently only about a third of people cook with their Halloween pumpkin.

This might change if more people knew that 100g pumpkin contains 170% of your recommended daily amount of vitamin A and just 0.1g of fat. It's also a great source of potassium.

How to prepare your pumpkin

Pumpkin can be eaten whole (roasted) and it can be grated. However, most of the recipes in this book call for it to be cooked one of two ways:

Pumpkin purée

Make a large batch of purée using an entire pumpkin and either keep it in the fridge for a few days to use as required, or freeze it in batches. You can often make multiple recipes from the purée of just one pumpkin.

Cut the pumpkin into quarters, remove the seeds and gungy bits and then put the quarters skin side down on a roasting tray. Cook in a pre-heated oven at 190C for about 45 minutes until the flesh is soft (stick a knife into it to test). Leave until cool enough to handle. Then scrape the flesh away from the skin (easiest using a metal ice cream scoop or metal spoon). Blend or mash until smooth.

Depending on the pumpkin or squash variety you are using, the purée may be very wet, which can sometimes cause difficulties. For example, if making falafels with very wet purée they will take far longer to bake. If you leave the sliced pumpkin roasting for a little longer it will dry the pumpkin out a bit to make a drier purée. If you are making something like soup this is not necessary.

Diced pumpkin

Simply cut your pumpkin into quarters using a large, sharp knife. Then scoop out the seeds and gungy bits in the middle using a metal ice cream scoop or spoon. Don't throw the seeds away (see seed recipes in the next chapter). Then dice the pumpkin either with the skin on, or after carefully slicing the flesh away from the skin, depending on your preference.

Pumpkin varieties

There are many pumpkin varieties, and even more winter squash. The pumpkin in all the recipes in this book can be replaced with winter squash, which are often even tastier. As a rule large pumpkins, such as those aimed at the jack-o'-lantern market, are more watery and less flavourful. They are still a good choice for a soup or for turning into a purée. However, smaller winter squash, which have denser flesh, often with an almost-buttery consistency and sweet or nutty flavour, are the most delicious for eating roasted. Given the choice, opt for a winter squash or small pumpkin over a large pumpkin (bigger isn't always better!) Some of the tastiest include (but aren't limited to) Crown Prince, Red Kuri, Kabocha, and Acorn squash. Pumpkins and squashes have the additional benefit of making beautiful autumnal displays. So you can display them at Halloween and then they should store for months (best kept in a cool, dark place) to eat as and when required.

STARTERS AND LIGHT BITES

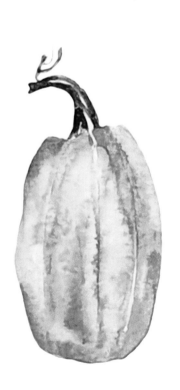

Roasted pumpkin seeds

If you like snacks such as peanuts and crisps you're in for a treat. Roasted pumpkin seeds are so delicious as a snack in front of the telly, or as a little pre-dinner appetiser. They are definitely too good to be wasted! You could also keep some seeds for planting. See below to find out how.

Seeds from one pumpkin
1 tbsp melted butter, olive oil or rapeseed oil
Sea salt

Heat the oven to 180C.

Either cut the top off the pumpkin (if using it for carving), or cut it in half with a sharp knife. Scoop the seeds out (using a metal ice cream scoop works well).

The seeds will be covered in pumpkin gunge. Put them in a sieve and pick off as much of the gunge as possible (you can add this to a bread mix if you like), then rinse them under the tap until they are clean. It's a bit fiddly but worth it.

Spread a clean tea towel over a plate or tray and lay the damp seeds on this to dry.

Drizzle some olive oil, rapeseed oil or melted butter into a bowl and add a pinch of sea salt. Add the seeds and coat well.

Lay in a single layer on a baking tray (lined with non-stick paper makes life easiest). Then roast at 180C for up to 30 minutes until crisp and golden. Check every 5 – 10 minutes as the cooking time will vary considerably depending on the variety. Once ready they will be very crisp, sort of popping in your mouth, with a lovely nutty flavour. If they have not been roasted quite long enough they will be chewy but watch out, they can very quickly go from the chewy to the crisp stage – and then burn. So keep a close eye on them!

Variations

The roasted pumpkin seeds recipe is simple and delicious. However, there are so many possible variations, in the same way that potato crisps come in many different flavours. It's fun to experiment with the spices and flavours you have at home. Here are a few that are tried and tested:

Sweet

Add a glug of maple syrup, golden syrup or honey to the melted butter and sea salt for a delicious gooey alternative. After roasting add a sprinkle of cinnamon.

Spicy

Roast according to the recipe on the previous page. After taking the roasted pumpkin seeds out of the oven, add a sprinkle of curry powder or garam masala.

Pumpkin pie spiced

Roast according to the recipe on the previous page. After taking the roasted pumpkin seeds out of the oven, add a teaspoon of brown sugar, a dash of ground nutmeg, ground cinnamon, ground ginger and ground cloves and mix well. Delicious!

To save the seeds for planting:

If you buy or pick your pumpkin at Halloween, you can plant its seeds the following spring. After cleaning the seeds in a sieve, spread them out on a tea towel and leave until absolutely dry (replace the tea towel when it is damp, and leave them on a sunny windowsill for a few days, turning them occasionally).

When they are definitely dry store them in an airtight container in the fridge until you are ready to plant them. If they aren't completely dry they will go mouldy, so err on the side of caution and leave them on the sunny windowsill for as long as necessary. Not all the seeds will be viable. Some will feel very flat. These won't grow. Those that are plump and hard are worth planting.

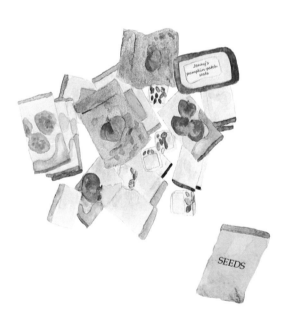

Pumpkin patch pumpkin soup

This is the pumpkin soup I serve at the pumpkin patch. It's warming with just the right amount of spice, and it's very popular. I like it quite thin but if you prefer a thicker soup cut down on the amount of water. You can garnish it with a little natural yoghurt before serving if you like.

Serves 4

1 onion, finely chopped
1 tbsp oil
2 tsp garlic, finely chopped
2 tsp fresh ginger, finely chopped
½ tsp curry powder
1 tsp ground cumin
½ tsp ground coriander
½ tsp ground ginger
1 tsp salt
750g pumpkin purée (see p. 16)
1 litre water (approx.)
2 bay leaves

Heat the oil over a medium heat in a frying pan and gently fry the onions until soft (about 10 minutes). Add the garlic and ginger and fry for another minute.

Stir in the spices and salt. Spoon in the pumpkin purée and cover with water until it is the consistency you require. Finally, add the bay leaves and simmer gently for about half an hour.

Remove the bay leaves and blend until smooth.

Pumpkin & chorizo soup

———··———

This is a hearty and warming soup perfect for autumn or winter. It's filling so could be used as a main course, served with some crusty bread.

Serves 4

Splash of oil
1 onion, sliced
3 garlic cloves, finely chopped
2 tsp ground cumin
1 tsp ground coriander
1 tsp paprika
200g red lentils, rinsed
400g tin chopped tomatoes
400g pumpkin purée (see p. 16)
1 litre chicken stock
Salt
200g chorizo, chopped into small pieces

In a heavy saucepan fry the onion in the oil over a gentle heat until soft (about 10 minutes). Add the garlic and fry for another minute. Stir in the spices, then add the lentils, tin of tomatoes, pumpkin purée and stock and season with salt. Bring to the boil and simmer gently for 30 minutes.

A few minutes before it is ready, gently fry the chopped chorizo (you won't need to use any oil, it will release plenty of fat) for a few minutes, then drain on paper towel.

Blend half the soup and leave the other half as it is to add texture. Serve topped with the chorizo.

Curried pumpkin fritters

These cannot be described as healthy, but as an occasional treat they are delicious. Crispy on the outside and fluffy on the inside. If you have a sweet tooth serve them for pudding with a ball of vanilla ice cream. Simply replace the garam masala with one teaspoon of cinnamon, a pinch of nutmeg and a pinch of ginger, then dust with icing sugar before serving.

Serves 4

100g plain flour
1 tsp baking powder
1 tsp garam masala
½ tsp salt
4 heaped tablespoons of pumpkin purée (see p. 16)
500ml oil for deep fat frying

Mix the dry ingredients together in a bowl. Stir in the pumpkin purée.

Heat the oil to 165C.

Add the mixture to the oil a teaspoon at a time. Do not be tempted to add larger quantities as the inside will not cook and will be sticky and mushy. Leave in the oil for about two minutes, until the fritters have puffed up and turned golden brown. Remove them using a slotted spoon and drain on paper towel. Serve immediately. These are particularly delicious with a sweet chilli dipping sauce.

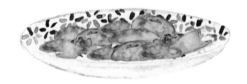

Pumpkin hummus

Hummus usually contains tahini (sesame seed paste), which is one of those ingredients I rarely have in the cupboard. If you don't have any to hand, feel free to make it without. Although it is tastier with tahini, it's still a delicious dip without.

Serves 8

2 garlic cloves
1 tbsp olive oil
500g pumpkin purée (see p. 16)
400g tin chickpeas, drained
2 tbsp tahini paste (optional)
Juice of ½ lemon
1 tsp ground cumin
Sprinkle of paprika

First gently fry the whole garlic cloves in the olive oil, until aromatic and lightly browned.

Add the garlic cloves, pumpkin purée, chickpeas, tahini, lemon juice, cumin and the oil from the garlic to a blender and blend until smooth.

Decorate with a sprinkle of paprika before serving.

Serve with carrot and celery sticks or bread sticks.

Roasted pumpkin & beetroot salad

When using pumpkin in a salad I recommend choosing a flavour-ful small winter squash if possible, such as a Crown Prince or Kabocha. I like to make a dressing using balsamic vinegar and the honey from our hives. If you can get your hands on good quality honey it will add a depth of flavour that you won't achieve with a cheap supermarket variety.

Serves 4

Half a pumpkin or squash (or a whole smaller squash)
1 beetroot
1 red onion
2 tbsp olive oil
A few handfuls of salad leaves
Handful of walnuts
Feta or blue cheese

For the dressing
2 tbsp balsamic vinegar
1 tbsp olive oil
1 tbsp good quality honey
Salt and pepper

Balsamic
Vinegar

Heat the oven to 180C.

Scrape out the seeds from the pumpkin and chop the flesh into chunks (leave the skin on unless it is a variety with particularly hard, tough skin). Peel and chop the beetroot and onion. Put them all in a roasting tin, drizzle with olive oil and season with salt and pepper. Roast for about 30 minutes until soft and caramelised, turning once or twice.

Place the salad leaves in the serving bowl. Top with the roasted vegetables, walnuts and cheese.

Combine all the dressing ingredients (shake them together in a jar with the lid on). Pour over the salad and enjoy.

Pumpkin falafel

These make a great accompaniment to a salad for a delicious, healthy lunch. Why not make them alongside Roasted Pumpkin and Beetroot Salad? Note the cooking time can vary depending on how wet your mix is (if your pumpkin purée is very wet it will take longer). These are quite heavily spiced but if you prefer a milder flavour cut down on the quantities a little.

Makes about eight falafels

300g pumpkin purée (see p. 16)
1 tbsp olive oil, plus extra for brushing
125g drained chickpeas from a tin
1 small onion, chopped
2cm piece of fresh ginger, chopped
2 garlic cloves
2 large slices of bread
Juice from 1 lemon
1 tsp ground cumin
½ tsp ground coriander
1 tsp paprika
½ tsp salt

Heat the oven to 180C.

Line a baking sheet with non-stick paper and brush with olive oil.

Whizz up all the ingredients together in an electric mixer until they form a paste. Put balls of mix onto the baking sheet using a spoon or ice cream scoop.

Brush the tops of the balls with olive oil and flatten them a little to reduce the cooking time. Bake for 30 minutes to an hour. Check regularly so they don't burn and turn them over at least once to make sure they crisp up on both sides. If the mix is very wet you may need to wait quite a while before they are cooked enough to turn them without falling apart.

Serve immediately. These can be frozen and reheated.

Pumpkin, blue cheese & walnut toastie

The walnuts add a lovely crunch to this toastie. I enjoy a strong blue cheese flavour but if you find it a bit overpowering you could use half blue cheese and half Cheddar.

Makes one toastie

2 slices of bread (any type of bread)
Butter
1 tbsp pumpkin purée (see p. 16)
3 slices of blue cheese
3 walnut halves

Heat up your toastie maker. Butter the outsides of the bread, then turn the slices over so the buttered sides are facing down. Spread the pumpkin purée on one piece of bread, top with the cheese. Break up the walnuts a little and put these in with the cheese. Then cover with the other slice of bread and put in the toastie maker for a few minutes. Yum!

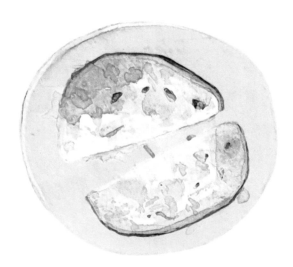

MAIN COURSES

Lamb & pumpkin tagine

In this hearty, wholesome meal the pumpkin soaks up all the delicious spices, giving it the most incredible flavour. Unless the pumpkin or squash you are using has a particularly thick, tough skin you can leave it on instead of peeling it. This adds to the nutritional value of the meal and also helps hold the pieces of chopped pumpkin intact, so they don't turn to mush during the cooking process.

Serves 5

800g diced lamb
2 tsp paprika
½ tsp ground turmeric
1 tsp ground cumin
¼ tsp cayenne pepper
1 tsp ground cinnamon (or 1 cinnamon stick)
¼ tsp ground cloves
½ tsp ground cardamom
1 tsp salt
½ tsp ground ginger
¾ tsp ground coriander
1 tbsp oil
2 onions, chopped
600g pumpkin, chopped

4 garlic cloves
1 tbsp fresh ginger, finely chopped
400ml chicken stock
2 tbsp tomato purée
1 tbsp honey

Mix all the dry spices and salt together in a large bowl. Add the diced lamb and stir well to coat the meat. Leave to marinate for as long as possible (overnight is ideal, or at least a few hours if possible but if you don't have time, don't worry it will still be delicious!).

Heat the oven to 165C.

Heat the oil in a heavy casserole dish and fry the diced lamb until browned. Remove with a slotted spoon and put to one side. Gently fry the onions until soft (about five minutes) in the casserole dish, add the garlic, ginger and diced pumpkin and fry for a minute more. Return the lamb to the pot. Add the stock, tomato purée and honey. Bring to a gentle simmer, stirring a little. Put the lid on the dish, transfer to the oven and leave to slow cook for two to three hours, until the lamb is tender. Check occasionally and add a little more stock if it dries out. Serve with rice or couscous.

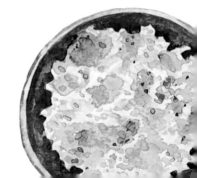

Pumpkin, pancetta & sage risotto

Pumpkin, pancetta and sage are a lovely flavour combination. Adding wine gives a depth of flavour but if you don't have wine to hand you can replace it with a little extra stock. Similarly, bacon or lardons make a good substitute for pancetta.

Serves 4

1 tbsp oil and 1 tbsp butter

The flesh of 1 small pumpkin or squash (or half a large), peeled and diced into 1cm chunks

1 large onion, diced

4 garlic cloves, finely chopped

200g risotto rice

100ml white wine (optional)

600ml vegetable stock (a stock cube is fine, but if you have homemade stock that is even better)

10 fresh sage leaves, chopped

80g Parmesan, grated (or strong Cheddar)

1 pack of pancetta / bacon / lardons

Melt the oil and butter in a heavy-based pan such as a casserole pot. Gently fry the onion until soft but not browned (about five minutes). Add the pumpkin and fry for a few minutes. Add the garlic and fry for a minute more. Add the risotto rice and stir to coat in the buttery mix. Pour in the wine if using and turn up the heat a little so it bubbles and reduces. Stir constantly to avoid sticking. Little by little add the stock, stirring very regularly. Wait until it has almost been absorbed before pouring in a little more. This will take about 20 minutes. You may not need all the stock, or you may need a little more. Once the risotto is soft but still has a little bite it is ready. By this time the pumpkin will also be soft but should still hold its shape.

Towards the end of the process fry the pancetta until crisp.

Once the risotto rice has cooked, add the chopped sage and stir in the Parmesan. Cheddar will make a passable substitute if you don't have Parmesan. Serve topped with the crisped pancetta.

Pumpkin, red onion & chorizo pizza

This pizza uses pumpkin purée and slices of roasted pumpkin. If you are a really big fan of pumpkin you could even put it in the pizza base – just add a tablespoon of purée into your usual pizza base mix.

Serves 4

4 pizza bases (home-made or shop bought)
Half a small pumpkin
1 red onion
Olive oil
½ tsp salt
8 tbsp pumpkin purée (see p. 16)
4 tbsp tomato passata
4 garlic cloves, peeled and finely chopped or crushed
1 red pepper
240g Mozzarella
80g Parmesan
120g strong Cheddar
200g chorizo

Heat the oven to 180C.

Cut the pumpkin half into four small pieces and remove the seeds. You can either peel the skin or leave it on. It is really nutritious so it's a good idea to leave it on, as long as the pumpkin variety does not have a very tough, hard skin. Cut the red onion into quarters. Drizzle with a small amount of olive oil and sprinkle with salt, then roast in the oven for 15 – 20 minutes until slightly brown. Remove and leave until cool enough to handle. Then cut the pumpkin and onion into thin slices.

Put the pizza base on a pizza tray or baking sheet (wipe the tray with a little oil to stop it sticking). Mix the pumpkin purée, passata and garlic and spread the mix on top of the pizza base. Cut the red pepper in half, remove the seeds and then slice it into long strips about ½ cm wide. Drain the Mozzarella and cut it into chunks. Decorate the top of the pizza with the red pepper, pumpkin slices, onion slices, Mozzarella and slices of chorizo. Grate the Parmesan and Cheddar over the other toppings.

Turn the oven up to 220C. Bake the pizza for 15 – 30 minutes (it will be shorter if you are using a shop-bought pizza base and longer if you are using home-made dough).

Pumpkin, bacon & cheese pasties

A very easy-to-make and delicious crowd-pleaser of a meal. We usually eat them with a big pile of baked beans! I like to make them with blue cheese, but you can use whichever cheese you like best. A lot of the flavour in these pasties comes from the cheese, so using your favourite will guarantee you like them!

Makes six pasties

For the pastry
500g strong white bread flour (not plain flour)
250g cold butter
175ml very cold water

For the filling
300g pumpkin or squash, diced
300g potato, peeled and diced
1 onion, diced
240g pack of smoked bacon
200g cheese, cut into cubes (blue cheese and mature Cheddar both work well)
1 egg, beaten

Heat the oven to 170C.

First make the pastry by rubbing the cold butter into the flour until it resembles coarse breadcrumbs (I just whizz it in a food mixer). Then bring it together with the cold water. Shape it into a ball and put it in the fridge until you are ready to use it.

While the pastry is chilling, cut up the pumpkin (remove the seeds first but there is no need to peel it unless the skin is particularly hard and tough), potatoes and onion. Fry the bacon and leave to drain on kitchen roll. Break or cut it into small pieces. Cut up the cheese into small cubes.

Roll the pastry into a long sausage shape and cut into six pieces of roughly equal size. Roll out one at a time into a circle, about the size of a side plate. Place a large spoonful of the vegetables into the middle of the circle. Add in some of the bacon and cheese. Then fold the circle of pastry over the top of the filling.

Crimp the edges by folding them back on themselves and pressing down with the edge of your thumb. Make sure they are well sealed. Then wash the pasties with beaten egg before baking for about 50 minutes, until golden brown.

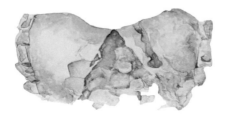

Pumpkin, chickpea & coconut curry

The beauty of this dish is in the mix of spices. Even my meat-loving husband says this is his favourite curry!

Serves 4

1 tbsp sunflower oil
1 onion, finely chopped
4 garlic cloves, finely chopped
1 heaped tsp fresh ginger, finely chopped
1 cinnamon stick
1 tsp mustard seeds
1 tsp ground turmeric
2 tsp ground coriander
2 tsp ground cumin
2 tsp garam masala
½ tsp chilli powder (or more if you like it spicy)
1 tsp salt
400ml tin coconut milk
600g pumpkin, peeled and cut into 2cm cubes
400g tin chickpeas, drained

Heat the oil in a heavy based pan and gently fry the onions, stirring, for about five minutes, until soft. Add the garlic and ginger and fry for another minute. Add the cinnamon stick, the rest of the spices and salt, and stir well. Add 1 tbsp water and allow the spices to infuse for about a minute, stirring, so that they form a paste at the bottom of the pan. Pour in the coconut milk, then add the pumpkin. Put the lid on and simmer for 25 minutes, stirring occasionally. Add the chickpeas and cook for another five minutes. Serve with rice and nan breads.

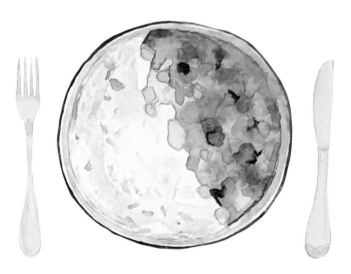

Cinderella in her carriage

Think toad in the hole, but in this case the sausage is Cinderella and she is in her pumpkin carriage! This is one of the most fun and exciting recipes in the book because a whole meal fits inside a pumpkin. It has the wow factor, it's delicious and it is also deceptively easy to make. For a vegetarian alternative just leave out the sausages!

Serves 4 generously

1 medium sized pumpkin (about 15cm diameter)
180g rice (wild rice if possible as this adds a lovely flavour)
A drizzle of oil
1 small onion, diced
125g mushrooms, chopped
3 garlic cloves, finely chopped
6 sausages chopped into chunks
80g pecans, toasted, or a handful of cooked chestnuts, chopped
150g spinach or kale, blanched
A handful of grated Cheddar
A small bunch of chopped parsley or 8 chopped sage leaves

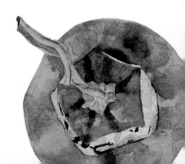

Heat the oven to 180C.

First cook the rice. Rinse it thoroughly, then cover it with 300ml water in a saucepan. Put the lid on and gently bring to boiling point. Cook over a very gentle heat until you notice the steam has stopped appearing from the pan. Don't lift the lid during the cooking process. Once the steam has stopped you should be left with perfectly-cooked, fluffy rice. Put the cooked rice to one side.

Gently fry the onion and mushrooms in the oil in a frying pan for about five minutes until soft. Add the garlic and fry for another minute. Remove from the pan and set aside in a bowl. Fry the chopped sausage until cooked through and browned.

In a large bowl combine the cooked rice, onion mix, sausage, nuts, blanched spinach or kale, cheese and herbs (using your hands to mix everything together is easiest).

Cut a lid off the pumpkin using a sharp knife. Remove all the seeds and gunge from inside the pumpkin (use a metal spoon or ice cream scoop). Then stuff the pumpkin with the mixed ingredients. Replace the lid. Put the stuffed pumpkin on a baking tray.

Roast for about 45 minutes until the pumpkin is cooked (you can test this by sticking a sharp knife into it).

Serve by spooning out some of the stuffing mix as well as some of the roasted pumpkin flesh for each person. Enjoy!

Pumpkin pesto pasta

This makes a really easy dinner and has the added benefit of using the seeds and the flesh of the pumpkin in one dish. If you don't have time to roast the pumpkin seeds you can use a packet of bought pumpkin seeds, just toast them by frying them lightly in a pan before using them.

Serves 4

30g pumpkin seeds, roasted (see p. 20)
2 garlic cloves
8 fresh sage leaves
200g pumpkin purée (see p. 16)
Salt and pepper
30ml olive oil
40g Parmesan, grated
280g dried pasta

Scoop out the seeds from your pumpkin, clean and roast them. Add these to an electric mixer with the garlic, sage, pumpkin purée and season. Blitz until combined. Add the oil and Parmesan, whizz again. Meanwhile cook the pasta according to the packet instructions. Stir the pesto through the cooked pasta. Top with extra Parmesan if desired. Serve with a green salad.

Pumpkin, goat's cheese & red onion galette

This makes a scrumptious centrepiece of a light dinner or lunch. Galette is the French name given to a pastry base with a sweet or savoury topping. It sounds fancy but it's really very simple!

Serves 4

200g pumpkin or squash, peeled, deseeded, sliced into wedges
1 red onion, peeled and quartered
1 bulb of garlic, left whole
3 spring onions
100g spinach
150g goat's cheese, sliced
500g readymade puff pastry block
Egg, beaten

* * *

Heat the oven to 190C.

First prepare the vegetables by removing the seeds from the pumpkin or squash, peeling and cutting it into wedges (large enough that they won't burn to a crisp when roasting them – you can always make them smaller later). Peel and cut the red onion into quarters. Put the pumpkin wedges, onion quarters and whole bulb of garlic in a roasting dish, drizzle with olive oil and season with salt. Roast for about 20 minutes until the vegetables are starting to soften and brown. Remove from the oven and leave to cool.

Roll out the puff pastry to a circle about 35cm in diameter. Mark out a rough line two centimetres from the edge all around the circle, using the blunt edge of a table knife. Then fold the pastry at this line, to create a double-layered edge to the pastry circle. If it doesn't stick easily you can "glue" it with the beaten egg. Put the pastry on a non-stick baking sheet.

Cut a piece of non-stick paper into a circle to cover the inner area of the pastry, leaving the outer crust area uncovered. Weigh the non-stick paper down with baking beans. Egg wash the outside crust so it turns lovely and golden in the oven. Bake for 15 minutes until the outer edge has puffed up. Then remove the baking beans and non-stick paper, egg wash the area that had been covered up and bake for another 15 minutes.

Meanwhile, boil the spinach in a drop of water until soft. Put it into a sieve and squeeze out any excess water.

Remove the pastry from the oven. If the inner area has puffed up squash it back down with the back of a spatula. Decorate the pastry with pumpkin, onion, garlic (unwrap the roasted garlic from its peel), cooked spinach and goat's cheese.

Bake for another 20 minutes and serve immediately.

Gnocchi with creamy pumpkin sauce

*This simple and tasty sauce can be used over gnocchi, or over pasta.
It takes just 15 minutes to prepare and cook so it's perfect for a quick
midweek meal. If you are a meat lover you can always add bacon.
Just fry eight slices of chopped bacon and add it in before serving.*

Serves 4

2 tbsp butter
2 tbsp plain flour
200ml milk
250g pumpkin purée (see p. 16)
125ml vegetable stock using a stock cube (approx.)
Pinch of salt
4 fresh sage leaves, finely chopped
Finely grated nutmeg
½ tsp mustard
Handful of grated Parmesan (or strong Cheddar)

Melt the butter in a pan over a low heat. Add the flour and cook, stirring, for two minutes. Remove from the heat and gradually add a little of the milk to the roux, stirring constantly. Once combined, add a little more milk, always stirring. Return to a low heat and continue to add the milk little by little, stirring constantly to create a smooth, creamy sauce. Stir in the pumpkin purée, then add half the stock. Turn up the heat a little until the sauce starts to bubble slightly. Continue adding stock until the sauce is the consistency you like. Add salt, chopped sage leaves, grated nutmeg, mustard and cook for a few more minutes. Leave to simmer gently while you cook the gnocchi according to the instructions on the packet. Stir in the grated Parmesan before serving over the cooked gnocchi.

SIDES

Creamy pumpkin gratin

A cheesy, moreish comfort food that could easily be the centrepiece of a vegetarian meal. In my family we like it as an accompaniment to a roast dinner or lamb chops. The smell of sage wafting out of the oven as it cooks is heavenly.

Serves 4

1 large onion, roughly chopped
½ medium pumpkin, seeds removed, peeled and roughly chopped (about 800g)
5 garlic cloves, peeled and left whole
8 fresh sage leaves
A glug of olive oil or rapeseed oil
200ml cream (double or single)
100ml milk
100g mature Cheddar (or, for a fancier meal, Gruyère), grated
20g breadcrumbs (optional)

Heat the oven to 190C.

Put the onion, pumpkin, garlic and sage leaves in a roasting tin. Drizzle with the oil and sprinkle with salt. Toss well and then roast for 30 minutes, turning once or twice, until just beginning to brown.

Mix the milk and cream. Transfer the roasted vegetables to an overproof dish and pour the cream mix over them until just covered. Top with the grated cheese and breadcrumbs (if using). Roast at 190C for 30 – 40 minutes, until golden brown and bubbling. Blitz under the grill for an extra minute at the end if you want to get the breadcrumb mix really crisp.

Speedy microwaved mini pumpkins

It is surprising that something so fast to prepare can be so tasty. It almost feels like a cheat! This recipe is only really good for the tiny munchkin type pumpkins (the sort that are so popular in displays) or the really flavourful small squash such as Kabocha or Kuri. We eat these as an accompaniment to many dinners. Occasionally we have them as a snack! You could also serve them as individual starters. Jazz them up by grating some strong cheese onto them before putting in the microwave if you like, or a little crisped, chopped, bacon. However, they are delicious as they are with butter and seasoning.

Serves 4

4 mini pumpkins or small squash
Knob of butter for each pumpkin
Salt and pepper

Cut the pumpkins/ squashes in half. Scoop out the seeds. Put a knob of butter in the dip where the seeds had been and season well. Place on a microwavable dish and heat on high for about two minutes per pumpkin, or until the flesh is soft. Serve immediately; you can eat the whole thing, including the skin.

These can also be roasted in the oven, for about 15 minutes at 180C.

Pumpkin & sage bites

A bit like a stuffing ball, these make a tasty accompaniment to any meal and seem to be a real hit with children. They use the delicious combination of pumpkin and sage, which is a real winner.

Makes about 10

A glug of vegetable oil
100g onion, finely chopped
2 tsp garlic, finely chopped
3 tsp fresh sage leaves, finely chopped
250g pumpkin purée (see p. 16)
80g breadcrumbs (homemade or shop bought)
1 egg, lightly whisked

Heat the oven to 190C.

Heat the oil in a pan over a medium heat. Add the onion and fry for about five minutes, until soft. Add the garlic and fry for another minute, then add the sage and fry a minute longer.

Transfer to a bowl and add the pumpkin purée, breadcrumbs and egg. Get stuck in with your hands, mixing it together and then moulding it into balls. Alternatively scoop out the mix using a spoon or ice cream scoop. Place on a baking sheet lined with greaseproof paper and bake for about 30 minutes until golden brown, turning once.

Pumpkiny mashed potato

Mashed potato is an absolute family favourite and an addition to so many meals, whether served alongside sausages or as a topping for a shepherd's pie. Spruce it up with the addition of pumpkin purée to add a subtle pumpkin flavour and an extra health kick.

Serves 4

600g potatoes, peeled and chopped
A knob of butter
A glug of double cream
200g pumpkin purée (see p. 16)
Freshly grated nutmeg
Salt and pepper

Put the chopped potatoes in a saucepan, cover with boiling water from the kettle and boil for about 10 minutes until soft. Add the butter and cream and a large pinch of salt, then mash until smooth. Heat the pumpkin purée in the microwave for a few minutes and then add to the potato, along with a sprinkle of freshly grated nutmeg and salt and pepper to taste. Stir until well mixed and serve immediately.

Roasted pumpkin & root veg

A simple and nutritious accompaniment to any meal. You can make this with any root vegetables you have available. I love the flavour of roasted new potatoes but you can use roasting potatoes, parsnips, or whatever takes your fancy!

Serves 4

500g pumpkin, cut into wedges
500g new potatoes, halved
500g sweet potato, cut into wedges
1 tsp salt
1 tbsp olive oil
1 bulb of garlic
5 fresh sage leaves, chopped
1 tsp chilli flakes

Heat the oven to 190C.

Arrange the vegetables on a roasting tray. Sprinkle with salt, drizzle with olive oil and place the garlic cloves (unpeeled) around the vegetables. Sprinkle over the sage and chilli flakes and mix everything until it is coated in the oil and herbs. Roast in the preheated oven for 30 minutes until soft and lightly charred.

CAKES, BAKES AND SWEET TREATS

Perfect pumpkin pie

The most famous of all pumpkin recipes, and rightly so! This recipe will make a real crowd-pleaser of a pumpkin pie. The pastry is very crisp and the filling is sweet and creamy. Adding a spoon of good-quality honey is not traditional, but it adds another dimension to the flavour. Pumpkin and honey is a good combination!

For the pastry case
150g plain flour
80g butter
50g icing sugar
1 small egg

For the filling
500g pumpkin purée (see p. 16)
3 eggs
100g brown sugar
200ml double cream
1 tsp ground cinnamon
½ tsp ground ginger
½ tsp ground cloves
1 tsp good quality honey

Heat the oven to 190C.

Line a 25cm pie dish with non-stick paper.

Rub the butter into the flour. It's easiest to do this in a food mixer. Add the icing sugar and egg. The mix should quickly come together into a ball of fairly sticky pastry. Press the pastry straight into the pie dish, working it until it spreads across the bottom of the dish and up the sides. It doesn't have to be too neat and tidy! Prick all over with a fork. Then cover with a layer of baking paper or tinfoil and pour baking beans on top (I use dry pasta shells as baking beans). Bake in the oven for 20 minutes, then remove the baking beans and baking paper/ foil and return to the oven for another five minutes.

While the pastry is cooking mix the pumpkin purée, eggs, sugar, cream, spices and honey together until well combined. Pour into the prepared pastry case and bake for 50 minutes.

Leave to cool for at least two hours before serving.

Pumpkin celebration cake

―――――

This cake can have two layers or four layers, depending on how impressive you want it to look! For four layers simply double the recipe and use two cake tins. Be careful to let the cake cool completely before attempting to cut each cake into two halves for layering, as it is very moist and will easily fall apart when warm. It is absolutely delicious covered with a cream cheese icing and pecans. Too delicious; it's hard to resist a second (or third) helping!

100g butter, softened
150g dark brown sugar
150g self-raising flour
1 tsp bicarbonate of soda
1 tsp ground cinnamon
½ tsp ground nutmeg
Pinch of ground ginger
150g pumpkin purée (see p. 16)
2 eggs

To decorate and fill
200g soft cheese
80g butter, softened
100g icing sugar
100g pecans, slightly chopped

Heat the oven to 180C.

Line a 20cm round cake tin with non-stick paper.

Mix the butter and sugar by hand or in an electric mixer until well combined. Add the eggs and purée. Combine the flour, bicarbonate of soda and spices and add those to the mix.

Put the cake mix into the prepared tin and bake for about 30 minutes until a toothpick or skewer comes out clean and it springs back to the touch.

Carefully remove the cake from the tin to cool on a rack.

Make the filling and icing by combining the butter, soft cheese and icing sugar. This will require a lot of mixing using a metal spoon, to remove all lumps. It needs to be smooth without any small lumps of butter.

Once completely cool, carefully slice the cake in half to create two layers. Spread half of the cream cheese mix between the layers and half on top as icing. Then pile the pecans on top.

Lightly spiced pumpkin cake

Most pumpkin cakes use pumpkin purée but this uses grated pumpkin, which makes it even easier! It is actually based on my favourite carrot cake recipe, which I have tweaked for pumpkin. I usually bake this in a square tin and then slice into squares ready for elevenses or the school lunchbox.

Makes 12

175g sugar
175ml sunflower oil
3 eggs
150g grated pumpkin
100g raisins
175g self-raising flour
1 tsp bicarbonate of soda
1 tsp ground cinnamon
Pinch of ground ginger, ground nutmeg and ground cloves

For the drizzle icing
50g icing sugar
The juice from half an orange

Heat the oven to 180C.

Line a 21cm square tin with non-stick paper.

Simply mix the sugar, oil and eggs, stir in the grated pumpkin, add the raisins and dry ingredients. Pile into the prepared tin and bake for about one hour until it springs back to the touch and a skewer or toothpick comes out clean.

Remove from the tin and leave to cool. Cut into a dozen squares. Mix the icing sugar and orange juice and use a teaspoon to drizzle over the cooled cake.

Versatile pumpkin muffins

These muffins are not too super-sweet or smothered with icing. There's a time and a place for cakes like that but sometimes you just need something a little more every day and healthy: a go to snack for the children's lunch boxes or to enjoy with a cup of tea. The aroma of spice as these cook will fill your kitchen with the smell of autumnal goodness. You can add raisins or chocolate chips if you like but they are delicious without, or try any other addition you fancy (chopped pecans or cranberries would work well).

Makes 12

230g plain flour
2 tsp baking powder
2 tsp ground cinnamon
¼ tsp ground nutmeg
¼ tsp ground cloves
¼ tsp ground ginger
Pinch of salt
150g dark brown soft sugar
200g pumpkin purée (see p. 16)
2 eggs, beaten
125g butter, melted
50g raisins/currants/chocolate chips (optional)

Heat the oven to 190C.

Mix the dry ingredients together in a large bowl. In a smaller bowl combine the pumpkin purée, eggs and butter. Pour these onto the dry ingredients and mix thoroughly. At this stage add raisins, chocolate chips or other extras of your choice if desired. Spoon into muffin cases and bake for 20 minutes. Allow to cool a little before devouring!

Plump pumpkin pancakes

These are fat Scotch pancake or American style pancakes, not the thin French-style crêpes. Serve them with a drizzle of maple syrup, golden syrup or runny honey. If you're like my daughter you will also smother them in melted butter!!

Makes about 10
(if you are greedy like we are, double the quantity)

100g plain flour
1 tsp baking powder
1 tsp ground cinnamon (this makes for quite a cinnamony flavour, reduce this to ½ tsp if you prefer a more subtle flavour)
150g pumpkin purée (see p. 16)
1 egg
1 heaped tablespoon of light brown soft sugar
25g butter, melted
60ml milk
Vegetable oil for the pan

Mix all the dry ingredients together. Stir in the pumpkin purée, egg, sugar and melted butter. Gradually stir in the milk with a fork (or whisk) until smooth. Brush a frying pan with a little oil. Put a scoop of pancake mix on the pan. When bubbles start to appear on the surface of the pancake flip it over and cook for a similar amount of time on the other side.

Pumpkin cheesecake

This cheesecake is extremely moreish. It has a delicate flavour with just a little spice. If you want to make it look extra special, decorate it with whipped cream, chopped nuts (pecans or walnuts) and a drizzle of maple syrup, honey or golden syrup.

200g digestive biscuits
60g butter, melted
400g cream cheese
100g caster sugar
½ tsp vanilla essence
2 eggs plus an extra egg white
100g pumpkin purée (see p. 16)
½ tsp ground cinnamon
¼ tsp ground nutmeg

To decorate (optional)
Whipped cream
Pecan nuts or walnuts, chopped
Maple syrup, honey or golden syrup

Heat the oven to 200C.

If possible, use a non-stick springform cake tin. If you don't have one, any normal round or square tin about 20cm diameter will be fine but make sure you line it with good quality greaseproof paper.

Mix the biscuits in a food processor (or alternatively put in a sealed bag and bash with a rolling pin) until the texture of breadcrumbs. Mix in the melted butter, then pour the mix into the bottom of the cake tin and flatten down firmly until smooth and compressed. Bake in the preheated oven for 10 minutes.

Brush the baked base with the beaten egg white (this isn't essential but does prevent the base going soggy when the topping is put on it). Mix all the remaining ingredients together and pour on top of the base. Bake at 160C for about 30 minutes.

Allow to cool and then chill in the fridge overnight if possible (or for at least two hours).

Carefully remove the cake tin (run a pallet knife down the sides first to make sure it doesn't stick) and decorate before serving if desired.

Chocolate & pumpkin swirl traybake

This traybake looks really unusual and tastes great! Adding pecans gives it an extra crunch but it is still delicious without.

Makes 16

130g plain flour
½ tsp baking powder
½ tsp salt
50g butter, melted
130g sugar
2 tsp vanilla essence
3 eggs
30g cocoa powder
80g chocolate chips
100g pumpkin purée (see p. 16)
½ tsp ground cinnamon
Pinch of ground nutmeg
50g pecans (optional)

Heat the oven to 180C.

Line a 21cm square cake tin with non-stick paper.

Combine the flour, baking powder and salt. In a separate bowl mix the melted butter with the sugar, vanilla essence and eggs. Then stir in the flour mixture.

Split the mix into two separate bowls. To one bowl add the cocoa powder, chocolate chips and nuts. This mixture will be very stiff.

Spread it over the bottom of the prepared tin.

Then to the remaining mixture in the second bowl add the pumpkin purée, cinnamon and nutmeg. Pour this mixture over the top of the chocolate mix that is already in the tin.

Then using a blunt knife swirl through the two mixtures to combine them a little, creating a marbled effect.

Bake in the preheated oven for 30 minutes. Turn out of the tin onto a cool rack and slice into 16 squares. These are delicious served warm but also keep well for a few days.

Pumpkin scones (sweet)

— ·· —

These are flavoured with cinnamon and nutmeg, giving your traditional scone a distinctly autumnal kick.

Makes 10 small scones

225g self-raising flour
1 tsp baking powder
50g brown sugar
1 tsp ground cinnamon
¼ tsp ground nutmeg
¼ tsp ground ginger
½ tsp salt
40g butter, chilled
150g pumpkin purée (see p. 16)
1 tbsp milk (plus extra for brushing the tops)

Heat the oven to 200C.

Mix the flour, baking powder, sugar and spices. Add the butter (either using a food mixer or grate into the flour). Make sure the butter is kept as cold as possible. Mix in the purée and milk. Knead a little until just combined.

Press or roll out on a floured surface until about 2cm deep and cut out using a cookie cutter to the size of your choice.

Place on a non-stick or lined baking sheet. Brush each scone with milk. Bake in the preheated oven for 25 minutes until golden.

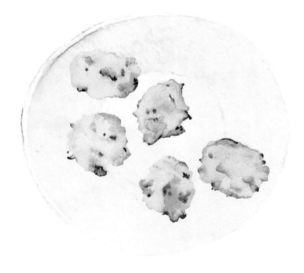

Pumpkin scones (savoury)

Use your favourite hard cheese to give these scones the flavour you like best.

Makes 10 small scones

225g self-raising flour
1 tsp baking powder
40g butter, chilled
150g pumpkin purée (see p. 16)
75g Cheddar or blue cheese
A handful of chopped parsley
A little milk

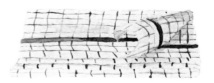

Heat the oven to 200C.

Mix the flour and baking powder. Add the butter (either using a food mixer or grate into the flour). Make sure the butter is kept as cold as possible. Mix in the purée, cheese and parsley. Knead a little until just combined.

Press or roll out on a floured surface until about 2cm deep and cut out using a cookie cutter to the size of your choice.
Place on a non-stick or lined baking sheet. Brush each scone with milk. Bake in the preheated oven for 25 minutes until golden.

Pumpkin bread

———·———

This is a pumpkiny version of banana bread. It's one of my favour-
ite recipes in the book: moist, flavourful and not too sweet.

Makes one loaf

200g pumpkin purée (see p. 16)
2 eggs
125ml vegetable oil
75ml water
200g sugar
225g plain flour
1 tsp bicarbonate of soda
½ tsp salt
1 tsp ground cinnamon
½ tsp ground nutmeg
Pinch of ground ginger
Pinch of ground cloves

Heat the oven to 180C.

Line a loaf tin with non-stick paper.

Mix all the wet ingredients together. Then mix the dry ingredients and stir them into the wet mixture. Pour into the prepared tin. Bake for about one hour until golden brown and springy to the touch. Remove carefully from the tin and leave to cool. Delicious served slightly warm.

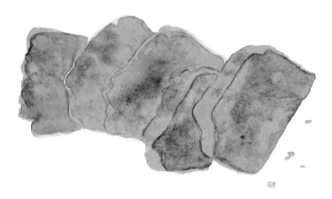

Four-way pumpkin cookies

These cookies are so versatile. You can have them plain, or add chocolate chips, raisins or nuts. My favourite is to add pecans, which add a lovely crunch and a more savoury note but if you have a sweet tooth go for the chocolate chips! If I'm feeling particularly generous I make a variety by dividing the mixture before adding the extras, to cater for the different preferences of each member of my family. They are quite cakey in consistency. If you are looking for something crispier try spreading the mixture more thinly before baking, but watch carefully to make sure they don't burn.

Makes 12

100g butter
150g caster sugar
1 egg, beaten
1 tsp vanilla essence
200g pumpkin purée (see p. 16)
250g plain flour
1 tsp bicarbonate of soda
1 tsp baking powder
½ tsp salt
½ tsp ground cinnamon
Pinch of ground nutmeg
120g choc chips / pecans / raisins/ walnuts (optional)

Heat the oven to 190C.

Line a baking sheet with non-stick paper.

Cream together the butter and sugar until fluffy. Add the egg, then stir in the vanilla essence and pumpkin purée. In a separate bowl combine the flour, bicarbonate of soda, baking powder, salt and spices and then add to the wet mix. Stir in the chocolate chips, raisins or nuts, if using.

Put teaspoonfuls of the mixture on the prepared baking tray, leaving enough room for them to spread a little. I find the easiest way to do this is to use a second teaspoon to scrape the mix onto the baking tray. Leave as mounds for a thicker, cakier cookie, or flatten with the back of the spoon for a thinner, crispier biscuit. Bake for about 15 minutes. Leave to cool for 10 minutes before removing from the baking sheet.

Pumpkin mug cake

This is a really fun recipe for children to make, or as emergency treat or pudding if you only have a matter of minutes to spare! Considering it is made in a microwave in just a few minutes it is surprisingly tasty, especially when smothered in custard. A word of warning – if your cup is too small the mix will rise up too high in the microwave and come pouring over the top like a volcano erupting. So use the largest mug you have!

Makes two mug cakes

1 small egg
30g brown sugar
50g plain flour
½ tsp baking powder
50g pumpkin purée (see p. 16)
½ tsp ground cinnamon
¼ tsp ground ginger
¼ tsp ground nutmeg

In a bowl, whisk together the egg and sugar with a fork. Add the pumpkin purée and dry ingredients and mix well. Divide between two mugs. Microwave one at a time on full power for 2.5 minutes. Serve immediately with custard or vanilla ice cream.

Spiced pumpkin gingerbread loaf

This is quite a dark, old fashioned sort of ginger cake, not the super sweet sort that you often find these days. I think it's absolutely delicious but if you want something sweeter replace the black treacle with golden syrup.

250ml pumpkin purée (about 5 tbsp) (see p. 16)
100g butter, melted
150g dark brown sugar
100ml treacle
2 eggs
50g raisins (optional)
200g plain flour
½ tsp salt
1 tsp bicarbonate of soda
2 tsp ground ginger
1 ½ tsp ground cinnamon
¼ tsp ground nutmeg
¼ tsp ground cloves

Heat the oven to 180C.

Line a loaf tin with non-stick paper.

Simply mix the pumpkin purée, butter, sugar, treacle, eggs and raisins (if using) together. Then mix the flour, salt, bicarbonate of soda and spices in a separate bowl. Stir the dry ingredients into the wet mixture until just combined. Pour into the lined loaf tin. Bake for 50 – 60 minutes.

Pumpkin French toast

This is a good way to use up a few tablespoons of pumpkin purée that you may have left over after making other recipes.

Serves 2

4 eggs
2 tbsp pumpkin purée (see p. 16)
1 tsp ground cinnamon
Pinch of ground ginger
Pinch of ground nutmeg
4 slices of bread
Butter for frying

Mix the eggs, purée and spices. Dip the bread in the mix until well coated. Gently heat the butter in a frying pan until bubbling, then add the coated bread slices and fry until golden brown. Serve immediately, drizzled with maple syrup.

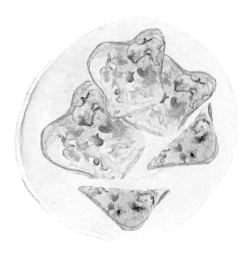

Pumpkin waffles

A quick and tasty treat for breakfast, brunch or snack time.

Makes about five waffles

120g plain flour
2 tbsp brown sugar
1 tsp baking powder
½ tsp bicarbonate of soda
½ tsp ground cinnamon
Pinch of ground nutmeg
Pinch of salt
2 eggs
5 tbsp pumpkin purée (see p. 16)
30g butter, melted
150ml milk

Mix the dry ingredients together. Then add the egg, pumpkin and butter, before gradually stirring in the milk to create a smooth batter.

Heat your waffle iron and cook until the steam stops. Enjoy with a little extra butter and syrup.

DRINKS

Pumpkin spice latte

This has become an iconic autumnal drink. It may not be a hit with the coffee connoisseur – but for lovers of a hot, sweet, comforting hug-in-a-mug, you can't beat a pumpkin spice latte!

Makes one cup

200ml milk
1 tbsp pumpkin purée (puréed until very smooth) (see p. 16)
2 tsp sugar
Pinch of ground cinnamon
Pinch of ground ginger
Pinch of ground nutmeg
60ml strong coffee
½ tsp vanilla essence
Whipped cream to serve

* * *

Heat the milk in a pan over a low heat. Do not allow it to boil. Stir in the pumpkin, sugar and spices. Make approximately 60ml of strong coffee. You can use a percolator, caffetiere or espresso machine but it does need to be strong. Pour the coffee into a mug. Pour the milk mixture over. Add the vanilla essence and stir. Top with whipped cream.

Pumpkin pie milkshake

The main ingredient in this milkshake is ice cream, just as it should be! As a result it is a very indulgent treat!

Makes one tall glass

8 scoops vanilla ice cream
8 tbsp milk
4 tbsp pumpkin purée (see p. 16)
½ tsp ground cinnamon
Pinch of ground nutmeg
½ digestive biscuit, crumbled

* * *

Put the ice cream, milk, pumpkin and spices in a blender and blitz until smooth. Pour into a tall glass. Crumble the biscuit on top and enjoy.

Simple pumpkin & banana breakfast smoothie

Tasty and healthy, this smoothie is lovely for breakfast and if you remember to freeze a banana the night before, it can be ready in a flash.

Makes one smoothie

1 frozen banana (mash before freezing)
3 heaped tbsp plain yoghurt
4 tbsp pumpkin purée (see p. 16)
3 tbsp milk
1 tbsp peanut butter / nut butter
1 tsp runny honey

* * *

Put all the ingredients in a blender and blitz until smooth. Pour into a glass and enjoy!

ABOUT US

Jenny Fyall

Jenny swapped a two-bedroom flat in Edinburgh for a 10-acre small-holding in rural Aberdeenshire in 2013. After a decade as a newspaper journalist, including as environment correspondent at The Scotsman, she started running a smallholding and pumpkin patch.

When embarking on the small-holding life, Jenny, her husband and their two young children initially bought two chickens. Fast forward to today and they have a large flock of hens, as well as turkeys, sheep, pigs, bee-hives and a field full of 5,000 pumpkins and winter squash.

A friend suggested the idea of a pumpkin patch after looking, unsuccessfully, for somewhere in the north-east of Scotland to take her children at Halloween. Udny Pumpkins was born in 2017 and now attracts thousands of visitors every year.

Jenny is an experienced home cook and enjoys inventing pumpkin recipes. She is passionate about using produce from the family's smallholding in the kitchen and keen to encourage everyone to cook with their Halloween pumpkin.

Annie Grant

Annie Grant is a watercolour artist from the north east of Scotland. Moving to Aberdeenshire at a young age, she quickly developed a love of the local flora, fauna, and wildlife.

Today, painting from her small home art studio, she is building a range of collections inspired by the beauty she was mesmerised by as a child.

Trained as a botanical artist with the Royal Botanic Gardens in Edinburgh, Annie's work incorporates both loose and controlled brushwork. Her style is delicate, luminous, and full of charm. Previous projects include being selected as the feature artist for an exhibition at Dunkeld Cathedral Exhibition, being sponsored to be an artist for the 'Oor Wullie' Big Bucket Sculpture Trail across Scotland (which raised £14,000 for the children's charity at Aberdeen Royal Infirmary) and being invited to be an artist in residence with the National Trust for Scotland Pitmedden Gardens.

Annie is hugely passionate about her work and hopes to share her vision to make every day a little bit more beautiful.

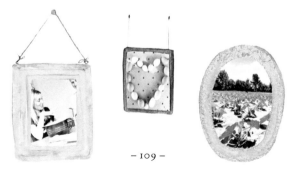